Within the walls

Cynthia Rodriguez

Instagram- @poetry.by.cynthia

copyright © 2025 Cynthia Rodriguez.
All rights reserved.
No part of this book may be used or reproduced in any manner whatsoever without written permission except in the case of reprints in the context of reviews.

Also by Cynthia Rodriguez

The Flowers Will Bloom

Becoming Spring Again

Table of contents

Houses

Stolen innocence

Obscurity

Winter's ghost

Mirror

Grief

Storms within

Nostalgia

Home

Within the Walls is a poetry collection about abuse, survival, self-sabotage, grief, mental health, and self-discovery.

Some of the things I write about are not drawn from my personal experiences directly, but rather represent my attempt to lend a voice to those who have endured such darkness.

It is a collection of both nonfiction and fiction.

Many of the poems reflect my personal journey and experiences, as I relate to the feeling of being lost in the dark.

The poems about abuse do not stem from my own experiences, but I wrote them with the intention of telling stories of survival, offering my voice to those who connect with them directly.

I want you to know: you are heard. I hear you.

These are the echoes that remain etched within the walls of the houses we have occupied—told through poetry.

Houses

Secrets hide in the walls.
Whispers leak through the cracks.
A fireplace that only harbors ash.
Floors that felt every crash.
Halls that lead to an endless path.
Rooms filled with paragraphs.
Ceilings that kept all the forgotten plans.

The house that you can leave vacant but will always occupy ghosts.

The house sits untouched for centuries.
Its only company is the memories.

All that the walls have seen
remains engraved within.

The walls heard every cry.
They felt the rage and the pain.

They saw strength die—
and strength regained.

They witnessed the dimming of her light,
and watched darkness consume her space.

But through it all, they sustained—
waiting for her home to be reclaimed.

The new residents open the door to their new house.

A draft greets them upon entry—
the echoes of all its history.

The house sits neatly polished on the outside—
white picket fence, a dog in the yard—
but it's all designed to conceal the truth.

Stories that were never told aloud.
Whispers that were silenced.
Secrets hidden behind closed curtains.

Cries left to echo.
Memories that won't let go.

A house that appears to sit quietly—
often called beautiful, but behind closed doors lives the unknown.

Ghosts don't only come after death.
Some still have breath.

And we end up haunted by the living.

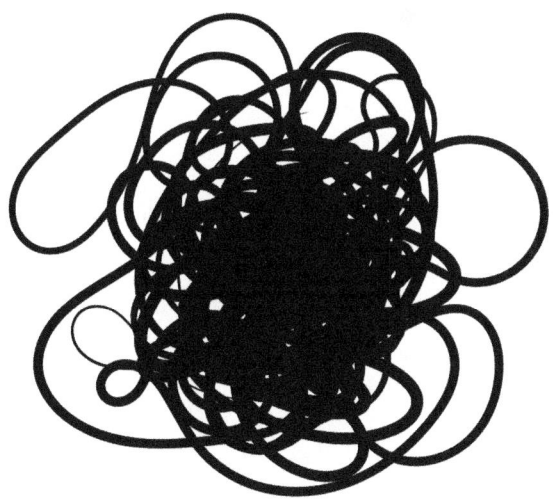

He extracted her childhood from her like a demon consumes the soul of a human.
And she should feel more empty, as something was taken from her,
but the absence of innocence bears a heavy weight.

*This is your new home,
and this will be your room,* they said.

They also said that would be her bed, so at 2 a.m., she's confused as to why he's in it.

He tells her she needs to share her toys or no one will want to be her friend.
Then he teaches her to share her body, proclaiming,
Sharing is caring.

And so she is taught that love causes an immense ache.

The other kids at school beam when talking about the love they have for their father.
And she hates herself for not feeling the same way.
She wonders why it doesn't hurt them when they share their body.

She only knows love as pain.
That love takes and takes.

And when she says she doesn't want it, he tells her she's selfish and she has to share everything because everyone else does it.

She's the little girl that all of her classmates tease for wanting to isolate.
The little girl who refuses to share her pencils,

because if she shares, then she will be loved—
and to be loved is painful.
And they will only demand she share more.

So she is scolded by her teacher each and every time, lectured on why one should share.

And she remains silent, because to speak is to go against everybody.

She was only a child—
but never knew what it meant to be one,
because her childhood was stolen from her.

Big hands were no match for her little hands.

He used his strength against her,
made her feel even smaller.

A strength that should have protected—

instead, it was used to damage.

Her worth was diminished.

And even in his absence, she felt his shadow
hovering over her.

Her skin mourns the absence of the sun today.
She sat by her window, waiting to feel its warmth upon her skin.

But the sun never came.

Instead, she watched the sky turn gray.
And the house remembered how it was raining when it couldn't keep her safe.

It knows that every time a storm comes, her skin turns red from her fingernails digging, trying to scratch the memories off.
It watches her become consumed by the storm's jaws.
It hears her being chewed by her thoughts.

And each time, it witnesses how the arrival of a storm haunts her with the cries of the night her innocence was lost.

She crawls out of bed,
bearing the weight of his entanglement.

He sleeps so peacefully,
while she's screaming internally.

Screams bang against her chest,
demanding to be let out.

Ashamed, she silences her pain.
She washes away his hands—
the ones that proclaimed her body was his to take.

She buries her wounds in that room.
But buried in her mind is the truth.

It refuses to set her free.

Her cries go unheard.
This time, it hurts the worst.

She asks, *why?* but never receives an answer.

She sinks into her own blood and tears, pleading for hours.

Pleading to the universe that one day, he changes,

that he becomes a father,

that he doesn't become a murderer.

That she may no longer be
a prisoner in his chambers.

She prays that one day, her voice is heard.

Memories of her eyes dry in that house are faint,
but echoes of her cries still circulate.
She entered that house innocent,
but she left tainted.

To this day, its new occupants say
they can still hear her footsteps.
Her voice is often mistaken for the wind—
until they step outside and are met with silence,
they realize the walls hold the noise within.

The cries and crashes cannot be forgotten.
The walls have been repainted, but the memories bleed—

the fake apologies,

the lost opportunities,

the forgotten itinerary.

All the agony continues to linger underneath.

The house that cracked and creaked,
not from age, but from grief.

They watched as lightning tore the skies apart.
The winds howled, loud enough to shake the heart.
The rain poured, desperate to leave its mark.
But they were not afraid—they were already used to the dark.
Their souls had already been scarred.

What they feared most lurked inside.
Behind closed doors is where the real storm hides.
The darkness inside surpasses the night.
That is where their fright resides—
where their hearts jump at the horrors of every sight, where their fears grip them tight,
reminding them to keep quiet or they'll ignite.

And nice and neat, they keep—like the perfect family.
Visitors assume they're too shy to speak,
but they don't see their mouths sewn shut, claiming their sanity.
People deem their home haunted by ghosts,
but it's actually their screams, so loud they can

be heard internally.

But in silence, they stay.
Standing at their window, they gaze—
watching as the rain soaks into rotten wood.

They become ghosts of their childhood.

Rain is pouring while we watch through the window.
Our parents warn us not to get too close.
We watch as the sand bucket we left outside overflows.
We stare at the clock, wishing for the rain to go.
The sky begins to roar.

But we don't care—we watch, noses pressed against the window glass, giggling every time our hearts jump out of our chests.

When our childhood was ingenuous, making us fearless.

And all we knew was innocence.

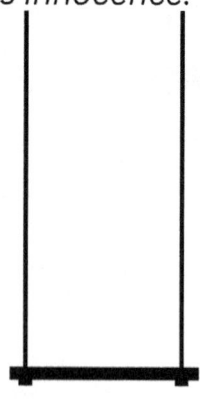

Hopscotch—we played until the morning rain came.
We modified the game.

Because it was ours.

And we were just kids—
novices to life experiences.
Yet we already had our bucket lists.
We were living in bliss.
We were naive to everything life would bring.

Because I still remember the day you came to me, bruised, pale face.
You insisted you were okay,
but you were never good at lying to me.

Because I could see the shift in your eyes—
from innocence to pain you tried to hide.
You bit your tongue till it bled, but I could still hear your cries.
And life's challenges had become magnified.
Laughter turned into dejected sighs.

And I miss when it was just you and I, playing till sunrise—oblivious to the trials and tribulations of life.

They begin a game of hide-and-seek.
She hides in the corner, in plain sight.
The other kids laugh at her.
She thought it was a great hiding spot,
because sitting there, she had always
gone unnoticed by her family.

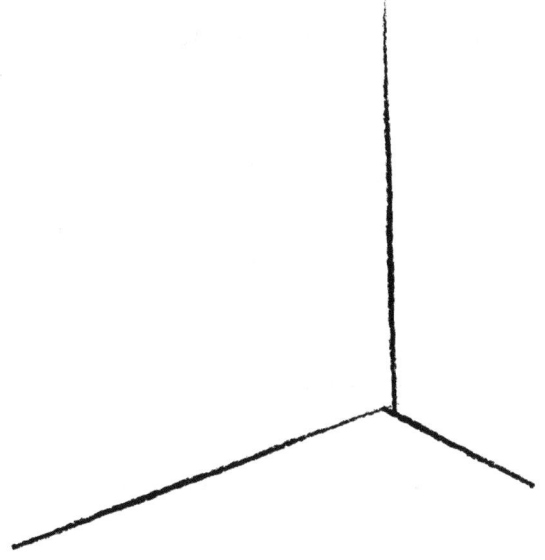

She hides in the corner behind a couch, forehead pressed against her knees.
She lets the tears stream.
Hands pressed against her ears, in hopes of silencing the screams.
She shuts her eyes, only to awaken unwanted memories.

One, two, three—she wishes to teleport elsewhere, but opens her eyes to the same reality.
But her soul—that one leaves.

She's the girl behind the couch, but she's empty.
Always unnoticed by everybody.
So she becomes invisible.
Her cries are only heard in an echo.

She's a prisoner behind the doors that always remain closed.

Four faces at the dinner table,
eyes fixed on glowing screens.
A five-year-old curses in victory—
he just killed a player in his game.

His mother shops online,
looking for clothes to create a new look to impress
the man she knows cheats on her.

His father schedules a meeting with the woman he
swears he doesn't love.

His sister giggles into her phone,
sending hearts to a man twice her age
who says he'll wait forever.

They chew. They scroll. They avoid.

Family dinners with ghosts.

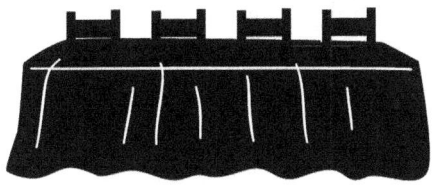

It's a breezy night.
The wind howls, sending falling leaves to brush against the window.

Winter has arrived,
and fall is saying goodbye.
She sends prayers to the sky
before saying goodnight.

But as the winds continue, the house begins to cry at the awakening of winter's memories.
There are happy ones, but there are also some that bleed.
And she watches as the blood reaches her feet.

She begins to feel the ache of winter
all over again.

Do you remember when you held her by the neck against the wall?
Because the house remembers.

It remembers how you only released her when her skin started to turn purple.
The floor remembers how you got on your knees, sobbing, begging her to forgive you, promising you'd never do it again.
But the floor remembers the weight of her frail body and your broken promises much more.
The taste of her tears and blood as she lay there bruised and bloodied each time you wanted to prove you were right.

The shower drain remembers how she tried to wash your knuckled fist off of her.
The mirror remembers the face of the woman it thought was a ghost, because her soul looked like it had died so long ago.
Even the sun remembers—from when she saw her through the south window,
a bruised, melancholic expression.
She was cleaning the window sill with a tremor in her hands.
The sun tried to warm her, but the trembling wouldn't stop.
The sun blew a kiss and waved, but even that

couldn't bring a smile to her face.

Do you remember her every time you look at the picture of you and your family on the wall of your brand-new house?
Do you remember her every time you kneel at Sunday's service?
Do you remember her every time you wash the blood off the knife you use to dismember the deer you hunt?

Do you remember her when you look in the mirror and your reflection tells you what a mockery of a man you are?

Do you see now that the sun belongs to the sky, and you had no right to take it?

He was a master at putting up a facade.
He wore the disguise of a good man all too well.

He knew how to keep her quiet, how to make her hide the pain.
He kept her in the dark.
An expert at concealing his wicked ways,
so much so even the dog knew when not to bark.

He was a man people could rely on.

But she knew him not as a man,
but as a dark force
hovering over her—

a storm that tore her from her roots,
leaving her without a home.

He tells you he loves you with words,
but shows otherwise with his fists.

And those are the bruised and bloodied hands
of the man who everyone says is *hard-working*.

They told you actions speak louder than words.
And you already knew—from the ringing in your ears—
every time he wanted to speak with his fists.

Screams rise from his chest and into his mouth, then he spits.

He spits his words onto her as if she were worthless.

He stands over her as if to prove his dominance, stomping on her self-esteem until it becomes nothing.

So much shouting, objects crashing.

But this is only part of it—

in that house, his fists are the loudest.

Dinner was served on the floor today.
First, it was set out on the table in a pretty teal plate, but he hated the taste.
It's too bland,
he complained.
Then he tossed it to the ground, sending the new dinnerware to pieces.
And she hurriedly rushes to pick up the mess.
She scrubs the mashed potatoes that landed on the walls while he slouches on the dining chair, his lips pressed to the bottle of beer.

You can never do anything right.
You're worthless,
he murmurs.

Earlier that day, a nice elder woman complimented her while they were both shopping in the kitchenware department.
She helped the older woman pick out a wedding gift for her nephew.
Noting the marriage ring on her finger, the older woman told her she was a beautiful, kind person, and her husband was lucky to have her.

Now she stands over the trash can, tilting the dustpan, throwing away the last hour she just

spent along with the compliments she received that day.
But his words—she keeps those.
Plays them in her head over and over again.

She feels as if a needle and thread are weaving through her mind, leaving every word embroidered.
And she aches for the walls that also have to endure the trauma each and every time.
She wonders how many times she can remove their stains.
Last week it was hot coffee, forced to kiss the walls for being too sweet.

In this house, she knows the walls see everything.

She tasted his bitter words in the living room for the very first time.
Used to their sugary taste, she was left dissatisfied.
Sick to her stomach, she began to regurgitate them right before his eyes.
But he picked them up, coated them with sugar, and fed them to her in spoonfuls.
And she consumed them as though they were a remedy.
The same bitter words, coated with
I'm sorry, but...

I'm sorry, but you shouldn't have dressed like that.
I'm sorry, but you shouldn't smile too much.
If you hadn't done this, then I wouldn't have reacted that way.
You look prettier when you're quiet.

The manipulation of
 It's your fault.

She's wearing her new red dress and her favorite heels.
But he's wearing the look of deception.

I like your black pantsuit better, he says.
Go change into that instead.

And when she insists on wearing the dress,
he tells her it's not flattering on her.

Red's not your color.
You don't have the body for it.
And those heels are too much.
I'm only looking out for you. I don't want everyone to make fun of you.

So she stands in front of the mirror again,
adjusting her black pantsuit—flats on.

And the mirror weeps—because it told her she looked amazing, but she didn't believe it.

She got used to tiptoeing whenever he was around, trying not to step on his jagged words.

They were in the kitchen, living room, bathroom, bedroom, the halls, and even her closet.

Whenever she reached into her closet,
she was constantly cut by the words:

Walking around her own home, she tried to avoid them, but she would still end up tripping over them.
And their blades would cut deep.

Once she stumbled over one, it was like the

domino effect.
Her blood was shed,
while he simply deemed her careless.

Well, you should be more careful with what you wear if you don't want me to say anything.

You shouldn't give your opinion.
Women are meant to keep quiet and look pretty.

You should really be more careful with your actions.

This outfit is flattering on you, considering your body type.

You're pretty when you smile.

Love the makeup—it makes your nose look smaller.

You're smarter than I thought.

The backhanded compliments.

She should have discarded the disparagement he gave—
but instead, she arranged his words into bouquets,
as if they were flowers, placing them in vases throughout her home.

The ceiling weeps because it was supposed to protect you, but it watched you drown every day.
It saw how his words became flames.
It kept quiet as you would suffocate.
The walls pleaded with it to open a vent—
but it was too afraid.

To escape is not always easy,
especially when not every part of you is in agreement.

Sometimes your mind is braver than your heart.
And sometimes your heart is braver than your mind.

Her voice was bruised from the many times her screams tried to escape, but she strangled them with her own recurring thoughts—

No one will believe you.
No one will believe you.
No one will believe you.

She was the light that lit her home.

But he dimmed her soul
just to gain control.

She was the fire that kept her warm,
but he was the ice
that turned her home into a storm.

She scrubs away the lipstick stains from the bedsheets.
She's always hated red.
Her husband loved it, but she never wore it.
And yet, somehow, the bed found the perfect shade.
But she doesn't say anything—she just washes it away.

And the bed knows that she made it,
but she's not the one who lay on it.

And she can continue to scrub the bed sheets clean,
but she can never erase what the walls have seen.

Broken crystals fall from her eyes—all because of the man who told her lies.
He promised her a greater love than the sun that lights the sky:
butterflies to enhance her life,
blissful memories to last a lifetime.

He also said she'd be the only one in his eyes.
You are my rose, he said
But soon, her petals would be dead.

Daisies would blossom, more flowers would bloom—
red, pink, purple, and blue.
Short or tall, he liked them all.
And he kept them a secret within the walls.

But the walls began to speak, revealing the infidelity.
The deception cut deep.
Many hearts split at his feet.
He smeared their self-love onto the floor, and their blooms became weeds.
But he still desired a garden, so he continued to bring new seeds.

He nourished them with love and kind words,

but it was all deceit.
They all believed they were the only flower he was growing.
But he had secret greenhouses in every room—
graves of the previous ones beneath their roots.

Because they died in that house.
Walked away in the flesh,
but he kept their souls—
buried their hearts.

And everyone always asks why his house is so cold.

It's past midnight, but she still sits upright—waiting, as if he'll come back.

Waiting for his knock.

But she never sees him walk through that door again.

She still sees him sometimes around town, with his new girlfriend.

But in her home, only his spirit remains.

No matter how many times you repaint them or change the wallpaper, the walls will always bear the memories of what they witnessed.

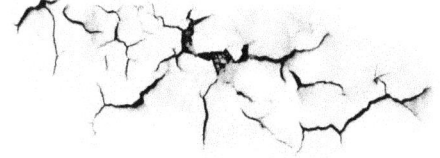

All the haunting, cracking noises heard throughout her house were actually the sound of breaking.

The ghost of every memory.

It's the last frost of the season.
Ice covers the roof, transferring its cold to the ceiling.

And the ceiling remembers the cold all too well.
It remembers the coldness he emitted, though he brought hell.
It remembers how his words would cause her heart to swell.

It remembers how she didn't love herself.

How she stayed,
despite all the harm he gave.

How she had the ability to walk away,
yet still felt there was no escape.
And it sees how her scars still bring her pain.

The cold causes the memories to unfold.
His shadow still creeps through the window—
refusing to let her go.

The ice outside always reminds with the chill of winter's ghost.

I shut the lights off,

close the curtains,

lock the door,

and pretend no one's home—
because I don't feel like pretending I'm okay today.

I hid in my bedroom to bleed quietly—
for I was ashamed of my wounds.

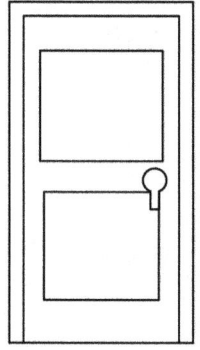

Who knew something so soft
could be so sharp—

whispers from insecurities.

I hear her whispers, her words taunting.
I wear a smile so no one sees her.

But she's there.

Self-doubt—she's hiding in the mirror.

The mirror cries at the words I speak.
Why can't you love me? it asks.

I've spent hours arguing with the mirror.
Wrote my flaws across the walls,
and had them recite them to me every day.

My home would crack each time—
as the floor shook with the echoes of my cries.

To not love a part of me
was to harm all of me.

Greed is a disease, and those who fall ill are not the only ones affected.

I saw greed feed off their desire for more.
I saw the hunger in their eyes.
Felt the impact of all their lies.
I could hear their monster growling from inside.

I saw them grow sharp teeth with an appetite for blood—my blood.
And they hunted me like a beast that, once it has a taste, must feast.

And I left them, but they had already marked me.
I can still feel the sting of their claws.
I feel their hungry eyes watching me through the walls.
And I hear their lies claiming new victims each time.
My home carries the ghost of my cries.

But this disease will forever haunt them—because to be greedy is to never be satisfied.

I held a smile beneath your cruel gaze,
hoping it was a mistake.
But you made it clear—it wasn't that way.
Your hatred would stay.

It was so different just the other day,
when you were asking me if I was okay.
You really made me believe what you had to say.

How quickly things changed.

You threw me into the lion's den.

For what reason?

Your fake empathy is an act of treason.

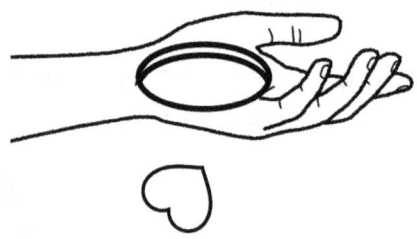

You offered me empathy in the form of a rose—
but you didn't remove the thorns.

I lay in bed, unable to sleep—
my eyes clinging to the ceiling.

I feel your words slither around me.
I feel your desire to coil around my body—
until I no longer breathe.

While everyone was grieving together, I remember
you came into my room, where I sat to cry alone.
You asked me if I was okay—
reached your hands out to me, giving my heart a
space.

Your words gave me comfort and trust.
Little did I know my heart would be crushed.
The deception I received from everyone else
wasn't as shocking, but yours shattered my heart
and bones.
I couldn't understand the hatred you showed.
You took my soul and tried to wring it dry.

Now I sit here remembering your words, as my
pain amplifies.
I remember your look of hate—
it speaks louder than any words you've ever
spoken to me.

And you never even gave me the chance to speak.
I remember you now as one of the reasons I lost
sleep—
how your hate cut deep,
and how you didn't care to see me bleed.

The only thoughts I now have of you are of you

as a wound.

And when that wound finally heals, it will become a scar.

And that is all that will be left of you.

I see you handing out your lies—gift-wrapped
real nice, ribbon-tied.
Pretty little bow on top, pleasing to the eyes.
And everyone's claiming theirs like it's a
prize.
But it actually comes with a price.

I bet they hear my cries through their walls
at night.
They sold their souls just so you could be
satisfied.
But there's no way what they did to me
doesn't still lurk in their minds.

And they can change houses as many times
as they want,
but the guilt will follow—
and always haunt.

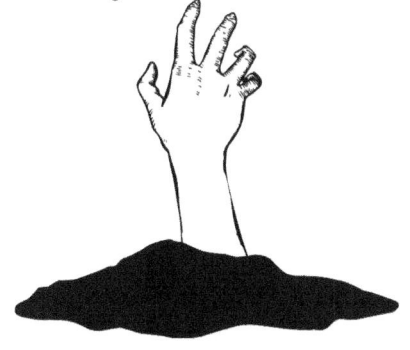

In this home, I've succumbed to many injuries.
But they weren't from fists or kitchen knives.
They were at the hands of people's cruel lies.
They used their words to cut deeper each time.
And people believed them—but I was innocent.

And the room felt the weight of my pain,
saw my tears become rain.
And I was drowning.

The roof lifted me as I was crumbling.
The floor sustained me on my feet.
The walls leaned in to embrace me.

No matter what they say, the truth is in the memories that will always be etched in this home—
and it refuses to let this be the death of me.

And as they dug a grave to bury me alive, they didn't realize they were the ones sinking—with every lie.

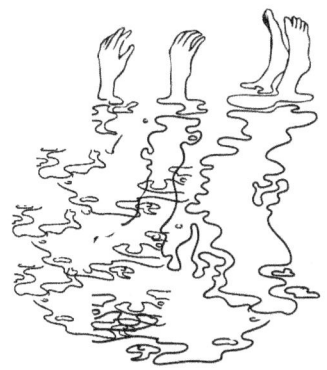

You feel the weight of their pain in the palms of
your hands, and you don't know what to do with it.
You want to lessen the ache, but your hands feel
helpless.
You want to give them all of your strength,
but it becomes weightless.

And to hear the sound of someone's heartbeat
grow fainter and fainter has a strength that
crushes.
That sound holds you in its fingertips,
squeezing until your hope is diminished.

You say goodbye to someone you love,
but then grief pays you a visit—
and it can never be banished.

I stare at the ceiling and remember how you had plans to remodel the living room.

I see all the places you wanted to go, and I feel the ache of knowing that door is now closed.

It brings a profound pain
to know those dreams are now ghosts.

The sound of a loved one losing breath
is one you can never forget.

I used to think people who were ill passed away in
hospital beds, drifting into peaceful sleep,
surrounded by family.

But life taught me otherwise.

When death comes for you, it can be cruel.

The chilling sound of someone you love
drowning in their own breath
leaves a haunting imprint.
To witness someone's suffering makes you
question everything.

No one told you it would be this way—
and even if they had, it still wouldn't have
prepared you for what you would witness.

Grief already carries a heaviness,
but seeing someone's pain adds a profound

weight of hopelessness.

And trying to bear it all leaves you restless.
It takes the light, leaving you only
darkness.

The sounds you heard
will always be eerie noises.
The shadows of those memories will
always lurk.
The echoes will always be heard.

To erase the memories of what you've been through
would be to erase you.

Your experiences have made you.
And although some of them are unwanted, to forget them would mean you'd also have to forget why you are who you are today.

Many times, I wish I could go back—
to reclaim moments,
to take away someone's suffering—
but I can't.

The memories are all I have.
Unfortunately, the good ones are also tainted by the bad.

But to forget would also bring pain, because the echoes will always be there—
calling, haunting—but they will be empty.

And emptiness can feel heavy.

No matter what they say, grief never leaves.
It becomes a tenant in your home that you can never evict—
a ghost you simply learn to live with.

I walk the halls of my mind.

I see the darkness consuming the last speck of light.

I was in a room full of people when someone said something to me that awoke the rivers in my eyes. I sat there, unable to stop the dam from breaking.

And as the room was flooding, the conversations continued.
Everyone else was floating, but I was sinking.
But not one person noticed.

I was invisible and alone in a room full of people.
My voice—unheard.

And I was swept away—
no one ever noticed I was missing.

You locked the door, but anxiety always keeps a spare key.

And it always shows up uninvited.

The doors are locked again.
She's banging and screaming, but it's to no avail.
No one can hear her cries.
She's trapped in the depths of her mind.
No one will ever find her here, as no one dares to enter.

She sits there, holding her tears in the palms of her hands, sinking into the floor that is barely holding the weight of her pain.

The air wrapped its hands around me and squeezed.

I tried to break free,
but how do you escape a grasp
you cannot see?

Its hands were not in sight,
but I could feel them gripping tight.

I begged for it to release,
but it continued to strangle me.

My lungs begged me to breathe,
but the air and I
were not at peace.

And I could hear my heart scream,
telling me I was actually in the claws of overthinking.

The grasp of your thoughts can have a strong hold.

Anxiety has a stubborn grip that refuses to let go.

I tell the wind to hush,
but it doesn't stop.

Instead, I'm met with never-ending thoughts.

They fill the room, spreading throughout the walls.
I watch as they cascade like a waterfall.

And the rain seeps through the ceiling.
Thunder finds its way in and lays beside me.
Lightning lights the room as it begins striking.

The floor cracks with the impact—
it feels the weight of thoughts from the present
and the past.

And my windows were closed,
my doors were locked,
but within the walls, there was a storm.

It made it inside—

because that's where it was born.

Bathrooms—
Sometimes used to wash your tears down the shower drain.
Sometimes we sit on our bathroom floor and contemplate.
We wipe the fogged mirror and stare at our reflection, wondering who we are.
Then we wipe our face and walk out of there like we're okay.

But the walls heard our pain, our cries, our heartbreak.
Within those walls, the ghost of us always stays—even after things change.

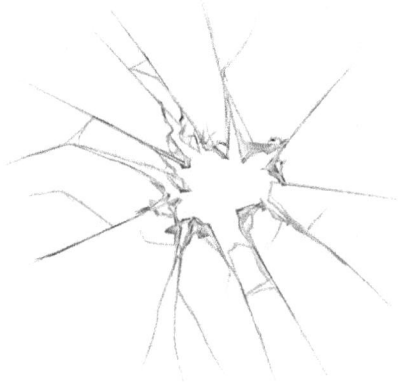

Mistakes become ghosts of their own.
You hear their footsteps,
their taunting deception,
the sound of the door creaking open when they're peeking in.

And you try to hide,
but they know their way into your mind.

In fact, they were born inside.

You push them out, but how do you get rid of what lives out of sight?

Midnights spent writing away my thoughts,
held captive by a mind that won't stop.

Listening to my heart vent.
Gazing at the moon through my window,
my pen still moving.

I run out of paper,
so I continue to write poetry on the walls.
The ink bleeds into the halls.
The ceiling recites my poetry.
The floor keeps asking for more.

The walls woke me up with their cries last night.
They couldn't take the pain caused by you
slipping through the cracks while they tried to hold you back.
And they continued to weep as they saw you
hover over me and demand I give you my peace.

They began to shake the room at the sound of my screams.
They heard me beg you to leave.
They saw me sink into defeat as I slowly let go of my tranquility.

My insomnia—
it refuses to set me free.

Dark clouds invade the sky tonight.
I sit in the company of the walls, who
tremble as we await the storm.

The room echoes with their cries.
They fear the memories that will awaken at
the sound of the rain and the wind howling.

They remember my pain as if it were that
very day—
the day my body refused to give my heart a
home.

The day I threw it out in the rain.
The day it could have been devoured by the
wind.
They remember how I locked the doors,
but my stubborn heart kept banging,
pleading with me to let it in.

And I didn't.

But it found a spare key.

On my bathroom floor, I sink into defeat, begging my soul to leave.
Unable to bear my thoughts screaming.
The pain weaving its way through me.
I warned it to hush or I'd make it leave.
But it continued to strike me repeatedly.

And so I went to the roots—my heart.
I had to excise it, as I was already being torn apart.
My body and my mind had already been separated.
And I left my heart to bleed.
But like a stubborn tree, it still had some seeds, and they quickly began sprouting.

I gave up, let myself wither away,
but my roots were still in there fighting—and they won.

Every thought of self-doubt was the rain
seeping through the ceiling.

My mind—
the wind, howling.

The thunder—
 my heart begging for mercy.

I created the storm within my own walls—
shaped by self-sabotage.

Why are you crying for him? I ask the walls

He was cold, selfish, and bitter.
How could you even miss him?

We don't, they replied
The door might have forgotten him when he left,
but we can still feel him lurking.
We remember his words around your neck.
The constant belittlement.

And we hear the floor cry—it says your emotions
are getting too heavy.
And the ceiling aches with shame for not
protecting you.

And you are not okay—you're just pretending.
We cannot move on without you or each other.
This house will crumble if we do not stand
together.

The ceiling, walls, and floor of your mind need
one another to remain a home.

One of the most feared things about anxiety
is that your mind never gives you a forecast.

There's never a warning—
you just find yourself in the middle of the storm.

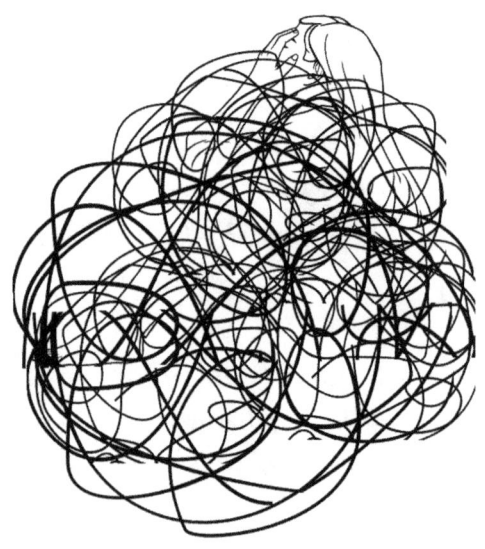

The mind can be a very cruel place.
Its floors can be unsteady, causing your thoughts to shake.
And it can lock its doors shut, leaving your thoughts trapped with no escape.
Its windows serve only as a reflection to remind you of your mistakes.
You try to get fresh air through the cracks, but it's a place that never gives and always takes.

As the walls cave in, you feel their crushing weight.
Your thoughts are screaming in agony, pleading for mercy.
And in the pits of your mind, you sit curled, knees to your face.
The rain seeps through the ceiling.
And on the outside, you can be smiling, but the storms are within.

Nostalgia

I heard your footsteps again last night, walking around.
But by morning, there was no sound.
You were gone.

Why do you come only in my dreams?
I wish I didn't only see you when I sleep.
I'm afraid to awaken, afraid to lose the memories.
I've already lost you once—the memories are all I have to keep.
If they fade, then I will lose you once again—
and this time, forever.

I don't want to lose the sound of your voice on Saturday mornings, telling me to wake up so we could go garage sale shopping.
I want to remember ten-year-old me—
even the sick days I now find comforting, as I remember your care, so nurturing.

And I know I can only see you when I close my eyes,
but there are always moments—little things that remind:
a sound, a smell, a taste.
Nostalgia will always be my favorite place.

To hear you sing again would be to reminisce—
reminisce the smell of cinnamon,
your smile in the kitchen,
the kitchen with the walls that knew you,
and even the kitchens with walls that never had
the pleasure of knowing you.

I can find the memories anywhere,
because nostalgia will always take me back
home.

In the kitchen, we laughed, shared stories, fed hungry bellies.
The kitchen saw love, but it also saw pain.
I often see the kitchen as a place where my mother often cried.
Sometimes I find it hard to sit there and enjoy a meal,
knowing it had become one of the things she desired most—
to be able to eat again,
to be able to keep down the little she managed to swallow.

To sit in your kitchen and be able to eat is a blessing.
And I feel guilty sometimes.
Guilty that when my stomach craves something, I can satisfy it.

The memories within these walls will always exist, even the ones that carry pain.
We just have to learn to live with them.

They tore the walls down.
The walls that remembered us now lie in dust.
The years of memories we built now vanish without a sound.
It was the home where we grew love and trust, my second home—the place where I grew up.

The place I knew my whole life, gone without a goodbye.

And so I ask:
Where do the memories go, when the walls no longer stand?

But they are etched in my mind, embedded through time.
The memories are not erased.
And when people ask me,
What is your favorite place to visit?
my response is:
nostalgia.

And I can go whenever I desire—
to reminisce about the halls I used to roam.

*You can lose the house,
but never the home.*

H♥me

When he says, *No one will ever love you like I do,* listen to your heart—
it's telling you it does not want to be loved that way.

When you're ready to walk out the door and it's raining, remember—you can always use an umbrella.

Life throws obstacles in your path,
but you can still keep going.

And it's always okay to ask for help.

You are allowed to tell people to leave.

You are your own home—
you do not have to open the door to those who only desire to come and go.

It is okay to refuse to settle for a tenant when you deserve someone who seeks permanent residency.

You can close the doors to those who harm you.

Let their knocks become ghosts.

You are a home worth returning to.

He tore her from her roots, but she found new soil.

Soil that nourished her, allowing her to grow into the best version of herself.

Arguments every day—
putting words where they hurt,
tossing trust out of the way.

They lost themselves inside that place.
And when they finally found their way,
they realized it was too late.

They decided they wouldn't stay—
and went their separate ways.

Their hearts were finally set free.
Their minds finally at ease.
And they never believed
this was the way it was supposed to be.

At first it was hard,
because they still hadn't figured things out.

But life carried on,
and they proved strong.

When you're lost,
letting go can bring you back home—
back to yourself.

She waved at the sun, as if greeting it for the very first time.

Winter's storm had deprived her
of its warmth.

But the sun had been there the entire time—
she just hadn't realized,
because she'd been frozen by the storm inside.

But this was her space, and she wasn't going to let him have it.

She lit a fire, and the ice defrosted.
The curtains opened,
the walls applauded,
the ceiling cried tears of happiness,
and the floor was speechless.

It felt like a birth was being witnessed.

And wrapped in a warm blanket was her heart,
presented with her new strength.

They had all missed being a home to the woman who had lost her soul.

Sometimes, you cling to the memories of your mistakes, just like they cling to you.

You pick at your mind over and over again, as if that will produce answers that could reverse the damage.

But it only creates more harm.

You can't get time back—
but you do have today,
and tomorrow,
and the power to move forward.

Silence does not mean you are weak,
but you deserve the chance to speak.

Don't let your voice
bleed.

A home should not be filled with rooms where your voice feels unwelcome.

Your voice is yours, do not let anyone take it from you.

You can speak your truth;
it will not make you weak.

You've bitten your tongue long enough,
silencing yourself.

You would rather have let it bleed
than express your vulnerability.

So, using your voice takes great strength.

Sometimes, letting go of the fragments you hold is what will piece them back together.

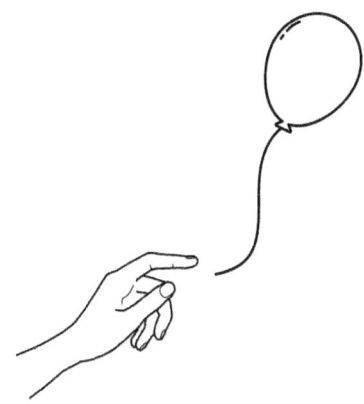

I was thirteen when a boy told me,
you're pretty, but you need to grow boobs.

At such a young age, that made me feel like I was incomplete—
like I could be the burger in someone's meal,
but never the combo.

And I believed that all the boys would choose the girls who came with fries and a drink.

And so, at ninety-five pounds,
I always desired to be one of the girls who fit those standards.
I stuffed myself with nutritional drinks.
Ate when I wasn't hungry.

But it was never for me.
It was so someone else could find me appealing—
so someone else could see me as complete.

But I didn't realize that not everyone has their burger with fries and a drink.
Not everyone is looking for the same thing.

To someone, you are already complete as you are.

When allowing love in,
remember:

just like when searching for a house to call home,
many may be pleasing to the eyes—
but be careful of what lurks inside.

Do not settle for a house that is not a home.

You deserve someone who will light the rooms of your home—
not someone who intends to keep you in the dark.

The moon watches as she cries from the midnight sky.
It cradles her through its shadows that peek through the window, trying to give her hope with its moonlight.

She tells the stars about the girl with a shattered heart—
how every night she watches her cry as she speaks to the sky,
how she can hear the echoes of her agony,
how she can see the floor tremble from the vibrations of her heart cracking.

She's the moon that wants to give her the sun.
She wants to give her daylight,
for she sees that the night awakens her fright.

She wants to tell her that even at night,
the sun is still reflecting its shine—
that hope never leaves.
Sometimes, it's just out of sight.

Sometimes, we speak harsh words to ourselves—words we'd never say to anyone else.

But self-sabotage is emotional abuse, too.

We create a storm that slowly erodes the foundation of our home.

Bruised by our own words,
we hide the shame with a smile on our faces.
Smiling like everything is okay is easier than
having to explain.
But it doesn't lessen the weight.
The mask comes off at the end of the day.

And we're left in the darkness of our own words.
Hiding pain is never an escape.
But self-love will always lead the way.

Love your walls.

Love your ceiling.

Love your floor.

You are also your own home.
You are also the home that has borne many cracks,
been through many storms,
and has even had repairs—yet you still stand.

Speak kind words to yourself—

she's always listening.

I hear her crying, and I tell her everything will be okay.
Not every war will be won, but I will always stay and fight with you.

Words I will speak to the mirror.

Your mind has held you through so much—
it deserves words that are kind.

Let love into your home,
but remember—
it cannot replace the love of your own.

Be at peace with the mirrors—
they are gentle daily reminders that no one
can replace the love you give yourself.

Imagine—
instead of taking in words that cut you,
you accepted the ones that act like fertilizer,
helping you grow and bloom.

To anyone who feels lost and defeated,
self-love is a map to find your way back home.

You have roots still fighting beneath the surface.
Despite what it looks like, you are not defeated.

I've seen even the most withered plants come back after a drought or frost.

Sometimes, even after their roots are removed, they drop seeds and continue to sprout new life.

And how could you not come back stronger after everything you've been through?

All your battles have made you a warrior—
even the ones you lost, because you built such great strength in fighting.

You could have bowed to the winds and rain,
but you stood—battered, cracked,
still reaching for the light.

To have sustained through it all took great
strength and courage.

And you thought you were weak,
but after every collapse,
you learned to rebuild with bricks instead of
straw.

Strength is like a home—
not born, but built.

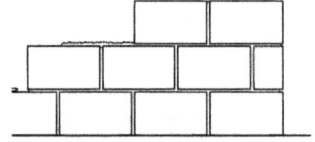

A home is man-made.
It needs you to build a strong foundation.

Sometimes, strength is disguised as survival.
You think you're barely getting by,
just surviving each time—
but that fight is you pushing an immense weight,
and you're getting stronger every day.

It's okay to choose to stay in the warmth of your bed, within your walls, for a day.

You're allowed to take a break from being strong.

Choosing yourself is not selfish.

It's a testament—
a reminder that you are not worthless.

The trees brush their leaves against my window, guided by the breeze.
I hear children in the distance, giggling.
The sun plays peekaboo behind the clouds.
Its rays slip through my window, warming the floor.

I watch the shadow of the tree branches from my bed, wrapped in warmth.

And I can hear her calling.
Get up, she demands
It's a new day today.

I told you spring would come.
The flowers wouldn't ache for the absence of their blooms for long.
I told you they would bloom again.
I told you your ache would be seasonal.

Now it's time for you to bloom again.

Conversations with the sun

When people ask me if I believe in ghosts, my answer is, yes.
The memories become ghosts—sometimes, even ghosts of us.

Every place carries something that will always remind us.
Whether it's somewhere you've been or not.
My home holds memories of me, but they also linger wherever I go.
Even the memories I choose to bury become ghosts in the end.

Whether I believe in actual ghosts or not,
I do believe that our memories are ghosts that will always remain.
Even if there comes a day when we don't remember them—
their echoes stay.

Houses—you try to leave them,
but they still possess the echoes of you.

Dear reader,

Thank you for reading my book. I hope you enjoyed it!

If you have a moment, I'd really appreciate it if you could leave your honest review and/or rating on Amazon.
Reviews help other readers decide whether my book is right for them, while also supporting me as an indie author.

You can scan the QR code below to be directed to the Amazon review page.

I'd love to hear your thoughts.

    With gratitude,

    Cynthia

www.ingramcontent.com/pod-product-compliance
Lightning Source LLC
Chambersburg PA
CBHW060321050426
42449CB00011B/2590